DO AS WE SAY THE NOT F

T0046088

SOCIALISTS

M.G. ANTHONY

Post Hill PRESS

A POST HILL PRESS BOOK

The Socialists:
Do As We Say, Not As We Do
© 2019 by Post Hill Press
All Rights Reserved

ISBN:978-1-64293-348-2

No part of this book may be reproduced, stored in a retrieval system, or transmitted by any means without the written permission of the author and publisher.

Post Hill Press
New York • Nashville
posthillpress.com

Published in the United States of America

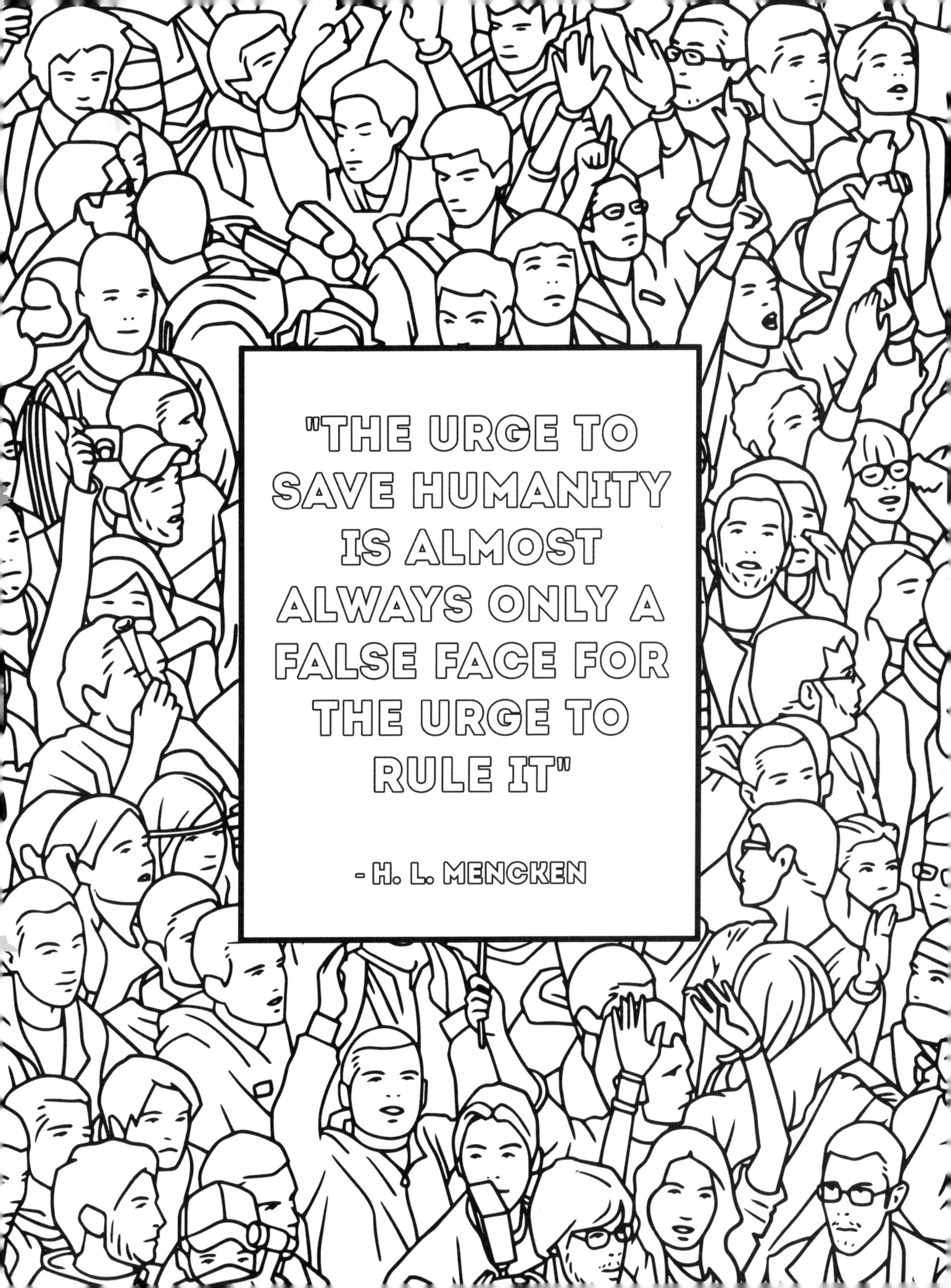
"THE URGE TO SAVE HUMANITY IS ALMOST ALWAYS ONLY A FALSE FACE FOR THE URGE TO RULE IT"
- H. L. MENCKEN

BETO
AND
BONEHEAD
SCREW
AMERICA
"Two Dumbs Up!"
- M.G. Anthony

CARAVAN
PELOSI

ELIZABETH WARREN
POCAHONTAS

Capitalizm

American
Toxic

GREEN
NEW D

IMPEACHES
MAXINE + RASHIDA = BFF
#TLAIBWATERS2024
WATERS TLAIB 2024

KAMALA
HARRIS FOR
THE PEOPLE

ROBERT FRANCIS O'ROUKE
FREE STUFF IN EVERY BOX
MAGICALLY SOCIALIST

POISON ALEX

VOTER'S REGISTRATION
VOTER'S REGISTRATION

RAILS
NOT
RUNWAYS!!!

SUBWAY
DEBLASIO

I DON'T ALWAYS
SUPPORT WALLS
BUT WHEN I DO, THEY
SURROUND MY HOUSE

SUPPORT
ISRAEL
HELLO
MY NAME IS
RASHIDA

Hey, Charlie, look!
Our boy Joe is at it again!